The Art of Floral Design

The Art of Floral Design

Paul Thomas

Original floral decorations
inspired by the patterns of nature

written by Jo Avison

WARD LOCK

To Marjorie Hoit, my grandmother, whose love
of flowers was my inspiration.

Paul Thomas

A WARD LOCK BOOK
First published in the UK 1998
by Ward Lock
Wellington House
125 Strand
London
WC2R 0BB

A Cassell imprint

Distributed in the United States by
Sterling Publishers Co. Inc.
387 Park Avenue South
New York, NY 10016, USA

A British Library Cataloguing in Publication
Data block for this book may be obtained from
the British Library

ISBN 0 7063 7672 2

Special photography by Guy Ryecart
Edited by Caroline Ball
Designed by Gail Engert
Printed by Wing King Tong Co., Hong Kong

Contents

Decorating with flowers, whether on a small or large scale, works at its best and easiest if you have nature as your guide. If you work with what nature has provided, taking your inspiration from the way flowers and foliage grow in the wild or in the garden, from nature's own colours and lines, from seasonal variations and changes, you will find arranging them hugely rewarding and enjoyable.

Each chapter concentrates on a different natural setting and looks at how it might influence the choice of flowers, foliage, containers and overall style.

Introduction

For each setting there are step-by-step projects which show imaginative ways of turning a source of inspiration into elegant and original designs.

The projects are offered as a guide, so that you can see how to take ideas from nature and adapt them to different types of floral decoration – using whatever is available to you. This will depend on the room setting, the occasion and of course the time of year. The book invites you to experiment with different types of flowers, foliage and mosses, taking your inspiration from nature and going where your imagination will take you.

The Alpine Meadow Bowl (see page 42) recreates the wide mixture of spring and summer flowers that cover the mountain pastures.

There are traditional rules of floristry such as 'the arrangement must be one-and-a-half times the size of the container' and 'every stem should be wired' and various other preconceived ideas that can be readily abandoned. Instead, you can train your eyes to watch nature and recognize its disregard for these man made restrictions.

Each of the seasons tells its own design stories, offering fresh ideas for combining colour and line, shape and style. In winter there are dark branches and bare twigs, carpets of moss, evergreens and flowering shrubs. The countryside's spring colours are clean and bright, with flowering bulbs and an extravagance of pale blossom and fresh green leaves. Summer broadens the palette with flowers in all shades and abundant foliage in all different shapes and colours. The soft pastel blues, lemons and apricots give way to the late summer mauves and deep pinks. As autumn takes hold, the woods blaze with fiery reds and oranges and colours deepen into the russets and golds.

This arrangement (see page 32) mimics the river bank and is designed almost as a stage set.

Hosts of ideas can be gleaned in the garden, as in the wild, from the gentle rambling of the herbaceous border to the disciplined shapes of the cultivated topiary garden. Even the potting shed and the conservatory provide inspiration and contrast; the one conjuring images of seedlings and wooden garden tools, while the other is reminiscent of exotic foliage and the brilliant colours of hot-house flowers from more tropical climes.

Though arranged with style, this spring basket (see page 108) gives a sense of blossom having simply been gathered fresh from the orchard.

There is little or no need to make your arrangements very complicated or elaborate. A few well chosen plants or flowers, displayed in a suitable container in a natural way, will often work much better for being relatively simple. The secret is to mimic the way in which nature would display them. In the meadow or herbaceous border, for example, flowers tend to grow in drifts through the grasses or foliage. Arrangements are most successful when they work in the same way, with bunches of flowers together in clusters, avoiding the overly careful placing of one stem at a time evenly around the centre. Flowers don't really grow like that and often lose their grace if so formalized. In nature, they are found together in clumps of a type, at different heights, with a sense that you could almost wander through them, discovering other flowers within the display. Creating depth is an important feature of many of the designs.

A natural order

Once the traditional rules of floristry are set aside, you have to be selective about what you use in any arrangement, to avoid being left with a chaotic mixture that has no definition and somehow doesn't make sense. There is, in fact, an order or form to how things grow in the wild. Consider for example, a bluebell wood. It has a pattern: a horizontal carpet of blue from which the vertical lines of beech trunks reach up to a ceiling of fresh green leaves. In all this there is an order, colours are not entirely random, neither are shapes. Even in the meadow, despite a jumble of flowers of all different kinds, the grass itself gives definition to the drifts of buttercups and white daisies running through it. It is this sense of natural order that you seek to reflect within the arrangements.

From a design point of view, this natural order is kept in balance by the successful interplay of line, colour, texture and shape, contributed not only by flowers and leaves, but branches, grasses, bark and moss.

Line

All types of design have used the beauty of natural line throughout the ages in many different ways. The imperial shape of the acanthus leaf in Roman times, the origins of the well known fleur de lis, the wonderful Iceland poppy that inspired the Art Nouveau movement at the end of the nineteenth century. In all these cases it is the natural line of the stem, leaf or flower that dictates the design – and you will find this gives vitality to your arrangements if the components are used much as they would be found growing. Rather than wiring branches or leaves into specific shapes or contorting them into downward spirals, use plants such as ivy or jasmine that naturally trail. Seek out contorted willow to create striking silhouettes rather than forcing plants into shapes they wouldn't normally grow in. Leaves wired into unnatural directions sit uneasily in their arrangements and will never look right.

Colour

There are many aspects of colour to consider in arranging flowers and again there is a kind of order to be found in nature itself. In the early part of the summer the meadow is a riot of colour – yet it is all held together by the grasses in their soft monotone green. Sometimes an arrangement works best with a limited range of colours, even using one colour or just several different

Wild flowers growing among field grasses create natural drifts of colour.

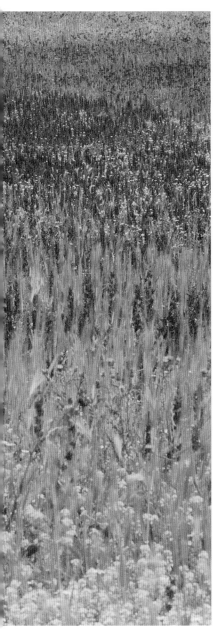

shades. Certainly nature has a way of using colours which create a mood from the sandy pastels and greys of the beach, to the vivid yellows and greens that tell you it is spring in all its vitality. Russets and rich terracotta colours, whether they are apples or roses, give you an autumnal feel and the success of an arrangement is sometimes in the strength of contrast provided by monotone flowers against foliage. Nature has a way of mixing the strongest colours together and making it work. The purple and yellow of a pansy or the bright contrasts in the petals of a gloriosa lily are stunning combinations that need little more than moss or foliage to offset them.

Texture

The glossiness of a leaf or the roughness of bark makes a valuable contribution to an arrangement, independent of colour or shape. In the planted arrangement on page 118, for example, the waxy gardenia petals are complemented by its own glossy leaves, and both are further enhanced by the entirely different texture of the jasmine's flowers and foliage. It is very important to keep an arrangement 'clean' so that the textures within it are not too busy on the eye. One way to do this is to arrange flowers in bold groups of each type. Another way is to play one texture off against another, by using moss, for example, as a background to other flowers. It allows their silhouettes to have clean edges and helps to prevent the arrangement from looking fussy.

The softness of rose petals is emphasized by the glossiness of currants or grapes and the contrasting texture of raspberries.

The texture of the container should also be considered as part of the overall design – terracotta, ceramic or basketweave will all show off an arrangement in quite different ways.

Shape

Shape, or form, has to be considered in terms of both the individual elements of the arrangement and the overall silhouette, including the container. The container is a crucial part of the design and must be chosen with the flowers so that the finished decoration works as a whole.

When working on an arrangement, plan the approximate finished size, creating in your mind's eye a rough silhouette, or the overall limits of the finished shape. Arrange the foliage in such a way that it comes near to your imaginary outline and loosely defines it. Always allow for some spontaneity and to a large extent let the foliage itself create the shape. You will see this principle throughout the explanatory steps for the displays that follow: the foliage is placed first, to be a framework for the overall design and provide a background to the shapes of individual flowers.

Flowers contribute three main shapes to a design: round shapes, spikes or spires and fillers. Some flowers may fall into more than one category, depending on the scale of an arrangement – phloxes might be spikes in some arrangements, but serve as fillers in a design as large the Majestic Summer Urn on page 80.

Using almost exclusively the round shapes of roses with delicate fillers gives this arrangement a soft, romantic feel.

Rounded flowers often form the focus of an arrangement and have a dual purpose. Used in groups they can provide the strength or body of the decoration and they are also the jewels, or highlights of the finished work. They can of course, act as fillers to some extent, however you will optimize their effect by treating them as a special feature with a major role to play.

Round flowers are emphasized by their immediate background and the juxtaposition of textures. The fillers and the foliage around them can play a crucial part in how they are shown off to their best advantage. Roses against alchemilla will look soft and romantic, whereas they will have more impact with the clean background of round fruits or dark moss behind them.

You will see, throughout the following projects, that round flowers are often used to give an arrangement its focal point, taking the eye into the decoration and adding to the three-dimensional effect. They are also used on their own occasionally, as groups of these flowers are invariably stunning in

IDEAS FOR ROUND SHAPES

lilies

dahlias

roses

gerberas

sunflowers

hydrangeas

peonies

chrysanthemums

OTHER SUGGESTIONS

agapanthus

carnations

giant alliums

NATURE AS INSPIRATION •

13

the right container. The Topiary section is a good example of round shapes working on their own, where tulips or roses are put in a hand-made container of box, to provide a clean background to the flowers.

Spikes or spears are used to define the overall shape of an arrangement. They give height and also provide a contrast to the round shapes. They can be used as a highlight when they are bringing a mass of colour to tall arrangements with lots of foliage, but their role is more usually to define the lines of the decoration and the outer extent of it. They help to create the structure, within which the round shapes and fillers can be used.

The herbaceous border arrangements (see pages 75–83) demonstrate how spiky shapes are used to define the decoration and provide an overall structure, which is then filled out with the other shapes.

IDEAS FOR SPIKES

delphiniums

gladioli

long-stemmed antirrhinums

bells of Ireland (*Moluccella*)

monkshood (*Aconitum*)

foxtails (*Eremurus*)

foxgloves

OTHER SUGGESTIONS

blossom stems

phloxes

stocks

Fillers, by definition, fill out the arrangement – however they are not just to be assigned to taking up the gaps between the foliage and other flowers. Fillers have an important part to play in creating depth and a feeling of three dimensions.

The fillers make it possible for the eye to almost wander through the decoration, behind and around the other shapes, effectively giving it movement. They provide a background of colour and texture to the round flowers and allow the spiky shapes to emerge from them. They do not all have to be used in the same plane in an arrangement – pushed low inside they give a sense of depth and vitality to the whole decoration as well as showing off the individual flowers.

Of all the arrangements in the book, the Majestic Summer Urn (see page 80) is perhaps one of the clearest examples of using these three shapes together. The spiky shapes define the silhouette and overall outline, the fillers create the depth and fullness and the strong round shapes of hydrangeas and roses are the highlights of the decoration against their background of alchemilla and foliage. It is a guiding principle that works and the invitation is for you to experiment yourself in juxtaposing one type against another to achieve different effects.

IDEAS FOR FILLERS

michaelmas daisies

alchemilla

phloxes

golden rod (*Solidago*)

spray chrysanthemums

OTHER SUGGESTIONS

september flower

dill flower heads

gypsophila

spray roses

Equipment

The equipment you might need is generally available and not many specialist items are required. Below are details of what was used for the projects in this book; many of them are household items.

Florists' supply shops stock a number of useful tools and pieces of equipment to make life easier. **Florist's tape** is used to keep floral foam in place and sometimes for hand-made containers. **Florist's bowls** come in a number of sizes. Made of inexpensive plastic, they make useful bases from which to create hand-made containers as well as lining smaller baskets. **Individual vials** and **extension tubes** are used in the wall garlands and in mixed planted arrangements to hold individual stems in water.

Florist's bowls (in a variety of sizes), individual flower vials and extension tubes.

Floral foam is available in many different shapes and sizes, including spheres, cylinders, rings and cones, but it is often easiest to buy blocks and cut them to shape. Floral foam should be pre-soaked (see page 22). Foam for dried flowers is a different formulation and is not suitable for fresh flowers.

Chicken wire, ideally with a gauge of 5cm (2in), is often used as a base for arranging. It should be crumpled to fit the container, without being too densely packed – there must be enough space for thick stems. Always ensure that chicken wire is well attached to the container (see reel wire).

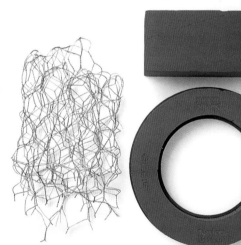

Chicken wire and floral foam (available as blocks for cutting to size or pre-formed shapes).

Wire in a number of gauges has many uses. **Galvanized reel wire** is helpful for holding chicken wire in place and also for hanging garlands or trophies as it is particularly strong. It is available from hardware stores. Where the strength of galvanized wire is not required, **reel** or **florist's wire** is generally used. **Silver wire** is used by florists mainly in bouquets and other fine work. **Stub wire** is sold in bundles; the size most often used here is 1·25 x 360mm. They are used for holding things in place, particularly for wiring fruit and bunches of dried flowers. Bent to form a hairpin they will secure moss and other small things without stems.

For cutting, make sure you have a good, sharp pair of **secateurs** that lock closed. They are invaluable for cutting the woodier stems and preparing flowers and foliage prior to arranging. Also have to hand a pair of sharp, long-bladed **scissors** for cutting raffia and the liner of containers etc. and for trimming moss and 'topiary'.

Raffia and **string** are useful accessories for tying hand-tied bunches and raffia can be used for covering wire or tape in hand-made containers. It is also a useful decorating accessory in its own right.

Black plastic sheeting is used for lining baskets and other porous containers, it blocks the light through basket weave and helps prevent any leaks. Lining is particularly needed where moss is used in an arrangement as moss can siphon water up from the container and cause it to seep over the edge. Heavy-duty household black plastic bin liners are a convenient alternative.

Where potted plants are used in an arrangement instead of cut flowers, **bamboo canes** or the smaller **pea sticks** can be pushed into the bases of pots to extend them and allow you to insert the pot into the arrangement as if it were a stem. Bamboo canes also help keep the base pad of a wall garland rigid.

A **glue gun** and **glue sticks** are essential for hand-made containers, so that moss and leaves, shells, sacking and other artefacts can be stuck on to an urn or florist's bowl.

Moss is very versatile and can be used to fill, disguise, cover and pack arrangements. Several types are used in this book: **Sack (sphagnum) moss** is used for packing and for making up garlands and frames. **Bun moss**, in the shape of little buns or balls, has a close, velvety texture which contributes a different decorative look from other mosses. **Reindeer moss** or **lichen**, in contrast, is open and greyish with a light, cob-webby look. **Carpet moss** is deep, shaggy and thick. **Flat moss** has neat growth that clips well to a flat, even finish and so is particularly useful for covering containers.

Household objects such as buckets, sticky tape and newspaper are invaluable. For a large arrangement, a **bucket**, preferably a metal one that won't buckle – inside a basket or urn is essential to support the weight of the flowers and foliage. Plastic **candle holders** with a pointed base will secure candles safely in floral foam, or **clear sticky tape** over the base will avoid the wick taking up water. **Newspaper, wrapping paper** and **polystyrene** all serve as packing to fill out the spaces between a bucket and basket or urn. In a heavy arrangement **gravel, stones** or **broken bricks** may be needed to stabilize containers.

Many other household items and collectables make useful accessories – candles, shells, pieces of driftwood, bark and dried berries have infinite uses; old pieces of china or pretty wooden boxes can be added to a collection of miscellanea to draw on for floral designs.

Clockwise from top left: florist's tape, galvanized wire, raffia, stub wires, electric glue gun, florist's scissors, reel wire and silver wire.

Clockwise from top left: bun moss, reindeer moss (lichen), flat moss and sack (sphagnum) moss.

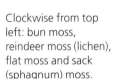

INSPIRATION

The Woods

WOODLAND BULBS

BLUEBELLS IN MOSS

FROM THE WILD

The River Bank

❧

MOSSY RIVER BANK

The Meadow

❧

ALPINE MEADOW BOWL

The Beach

❧

SEASHELLS AND CANDLES

WILLOW, WATER AND HELLEBORES

DAISIES IN MEADOW GRASS

BEACH WALL GARLAND

Imagine sunlight filtering through the bare branches of a wood in early springtime lighting up the new shoots emerging from the woodland floor. Dark leaves and twigs left over from winter contrast with the bright greens and yellows of first flowers among the tree roots, and a closer look shows the soft texture of new mosses against rough, gnarled bark.

By late spring carpets of bluebells crowd among the trees in wide drifts across the woodland floor. Although some branches are still bare, there is a veil of lime green forming overhead in a canopy of buds and leaves.

The new foliage and the flowers form horizontal bands of colour, green over fresh yellows or blues, and the newness of growth is emphasized by the aged tree roots – a sense of spring emerging through the forest floor. It is these elements of line, colour and contrast that provide the style for the two simple arrangements in this chapter.

terracotta drip tray
black plastic sheeting or bin liner
2 blocks of floral foam (pre-soaked: see below)
kitchen knife (to cut floral foam)
chicken wire
reel wire
stub wire bent into pins
fresh flat moss
potted miniature daffodil plants
trailing ivy
a few small dry leaves from the woods or garden
    (beech are a good size and colour)

PRACTICAL POINTS
This 20cm (8in) tray took three miniature
daffodil plants and two or three trails of ivy
with half a tray of moss. The daffodils used
here are called 'Tête-à-tête', but any miniature
multi-headed type would be suitable, as would
snowdrops or miniature tulips.

Woodland Bulbs

Daffodils, with their green and yellow freshness,
are the harbingers of spring. Before the trees are in
leaf the bright green shoots of wild daffodils pierce
the moss and ivy that litter the woodland floor.
By displaying the bulbs and exposed roots of the
daffodils, this arrangement recreates a sense of
bark and tree roots among the fallen leaves from
last autumn.

 Floral foam should be pre-soaked for
fresh flowers and foliage. Put in a bowl
of water and do not submerge it but let it absorb
the water at its own rate. This will only take a
few minutes.

1 Cut the black plastic large enough to line the terracotta dish with a 5cm (2in) overlap – it is essential to line the dish as terracotta is porous. Cut a piece of chicken wire roughly in a circle, a little larger in diameter than the dish.

2 Take a block of soaked floral foam and cut off the corners so that it will sit in the centre of the dish. Turn and roughly trim the corner wedges to fill out the spaces in the dish, until you have a flat block of foam that fills the dish base. Place more floral foam on top to give additional height in the middle.

3 Shape the floral foam into a mound by slotting offcuts of foam into the gaps and carving a domed shape with the knife. Curve the knife round and down as you work and don't be too concerned if the pieces move – just hold them as you work – the chicken wire will fix them in place. Once the mound is formed, lay the chicken wire over it and trim to size so that it meets the edge of the dish. Twist a length of reel wire together to form a ring slightly smaller in diameter than the rim of the dish. Stand the dish inside the wire ring, then loop short lengths of reel wire around the wire ring and the chicken wire to anchor the floral foam and hold it to the base of the dish. Work from one side to the other, attaching it in four places, so that the chicken wire is pulled taught down over the floral foam mound.

4 Cover the mound all over with moss so that there are no gaps. Use stub wire, bent in half to make pins, to attach the moss securely so that the pins are embedded into the moss and won't be seen. Delicately trim the moss by clipping the straggly ends with sharp scissors.

5 Remove the daffodils from their pots and gently shake off the loose soil from around the roots. Carefully wash the bulbs and roots clean of soil, taking care not to break any of the roots. Attach the daffodils by standing the bulb on the top of the mound and gently spreading the roots out like miniature tree roots. Hold the bulbs in position with two or three stub wire pins placed over the roots and pushed through the moss into the floral foam.

6 Take a length of ivy and strip the bottom 10cm (4in) of leaves. Press this into the moss at the back of the arrangement. Thread the ivy around the mound, securing it with stub wire pins as you go. Let the ivy appear to trail naturally, rather than wrapping it around in a formal ring, so that it undulates over the mound. Pin it so that the ivy leaves hide the wires. As a final touch, place a few autumn leaves randomly over the moss to create the forest floor.

Bluebells in Moss

YOU WILL NEED
plastic florist's bowl
chicken wire
reel wire
glue and glue gun
green moss
bark (small pieces no longer than the
    height of the bowl)
leaves, preferably quite dry
bluebells
bluebell leaves

There is something quite uplifting about the sight of drifts of bluebells carpeting the woods in late spring and shafts of sunlight highlighting the sea of blue covering the woodland floor. This very simple hand-made container, decorated with dry leaves and small pieces of bark, makes a perfect setting for the bluebells, displaying them just as they might grow in the wild.

PRACTICAL POINTS
This container used as its base a 20cm (8in) florist's bowl. The same arrangement could be created on a smaller or larger scale. The key design elements are to cover the container completely and to arrange the flowers as they grow in the wild – in drifts rather than singly. The container will dry out naturally and can be used for other arrangements or even be planted up with other spring bulbs such as hyacinths or crocuses.

1 Make a ball of chicken wire big enough to fill the bowl and stand about 5cm (2in) proud when pressed inside. Secure the chicken wire to the bowl with two loops of reel wire at right angles, taken over the edge and across the base of the bowl and up the other side.

2 Sort out flat pieces of moss and bark for covering the bowl. Using a glue gun, stick the moss and bark directly on to the sides of the bowl. Ensure the rim and reel wire are also disguised. Glue the leaves on top, but allow the bark and moss to show through, giving the feel of trees growing up from the forest floor.

3 When the bowl is completely covered, fill it almost to the top with water. Take bluebell leaves in small handfuls and push them through the chicken wire at intervals. Make sure the leaves are in clumps just as they might grow in the woods, leaving spaces in the chicken wire for the bluebell flowers.

4 Start to thread bluebells among the leaves. Work with two or three stems at a time, rather than single stems, and avoid placing them too carefully – you are looking for the slightly wild feel of clusters of growing bluebells.

5 Keep adding bluebells until the bowl looks well-filled – any small gaps where the chicken wire is still visible can be plugged with moss. Odd taller flowers can be left to 'grow' out of the arrangement, just as they might in nature and will give the finished decoration depth and interest, but avoid positioning them all near the centre, which will result in an unnaturally neat dome.

For this chapter inspiration is taken from a riverside setting of overhanging trees and mossy banks, where everything is lush and green. As you look closely, the leafy crevices reveal little clumps of pale flowers and corners hide small leafy plants and mosses among the stones. Along the river, tall rushes move in the wind and the hanging branches of the weeping willow trail in the water as if they might float downstream. The whole impression is one of light through the willow branches and bright clear water, glistening on the shingle at the water's edge.

It is the movement of willow through the water and the simple colouring that are captured in these decorations to recreate different impressions of the river bank.

Mossy River Bank

Made up of a mixture of potted plants, cut flowers and contorted willow, this spring arrangement is rather like a stage set of a riverside, mimicking the textures and patterns of the river bank itself. It is actually a very quick and easy arrangement to put together, as the plants all remain in their pots and the only cut flowers used here are the irises, hellebores and the stems of contorted willow. The secret is to keep the colours muted and retain a riverside feel by allowing the greenery to overhang the 'bank' and appear to grow out of crevices, just as it would do in nature.

YOU WILL NEED

black plastic sheeting or bin liners
small plastic buckets or flower pots lined
    with black plastic
2 blocks of floral foam
rocks
gravel and/or sand
assortment of low-growing plants such as
    lily-of-the-valley, primulas and their wild
    relations, primroses and cowslips
contorted willow (*Salix tortuosa*), just
    shooting
mind-your-own-business plant (*Soleirolia*
    or *Helxine soleirolii*)
moss
selection of cut flowers, such as irises and
    hellebores

PRACTICAL POINTS

This arrangement can either be put together *in situ*, or made on a board or tray and moved as a complete display. Use what moss, leaves, roots and rocks you can find, supplemented by a small selection of suitable potted and cut flowers and interesting branches.

Remember to place a deep cut – up to about 5cm (2in) – in stems of foliage and flowers to help them take up sufficient water. Woody stems will need to be cut about 7–8cm (3in) up from the base. The first 2–3cm (1in) can then be crushed with a hammer to ensure the foliage or flower will drink well and last longer.

1 Cover the entire surface with black plastic to protect it. Place the rocks where you imagine the water's edge will be. Fill two small buckets or flower pots with floral foam and place them behind the rocks: these will hold the willow and cut flowers. Bear in mind that everything can be moved – at this stage you are 'creating the set' so you can play around with the positioning of the different elements you have chosen.

2 Begin to place the pots of plants inside the shape you have created, letting the rocks designate the edge or border line. Imagine how they might grow on the river bank, and let the leaves overhang the rocks and the plants stand at different heights.

3 Place the contorted willow in one of the buckets or flower pots, making sure that it comes forward as well as creating the silhouette you want from side to side. This helps to give the arrangement three dimensions and the feeling of leafy trees overhanging the river.

4 Use the mind-your-own-business plants next, to fill the gaps in the edge of the arrangement. Leave them in the pots and stand or lay them on their sides, so that they bush around the rocks and really seem to grow out from crevices in a mass of layers. Use moss and more mind-your-own-business to hide the flower pots.

5 Add the taller plants and cut flowers now. Here the hellebores' flower stems have been pushed into the floral foam with the contorted willow, and their foliage added separately so that it overhangs the rocks. The irises were put into the second bucket of floral foam all together, to form a natural-looking patch. They have been threaded among the branches of willow to increase the three-dimensional effect.

6 Finally, the area in front of the arrangement is covered in sand and/or gravel to take you to the imaginary water's edge.

Willow, Water and Hellebores

The character of this arrangement is simple and clean, seeking to portray the movement of the flowing river, dragging willow branches along. Keeping the style fairly minimal brings out the twists and curves of the willow stems and the elegance of the flowers. To emphasize the shape further, the colour is almost a monotone green. The gravel in the clear glass vases recreates the image of crystal clear water over pebbles and shingle at the water's edge.

YOU WILL NEED
3 glass vases
gravel
contorted willow (*Salix tortuosa*)
selection of hellebore stems (*Helleborus orientalis*, *H. corsicus* and *H. foetidus*)
guelder rose (*Viburnum opulus*)

PRACTICAL POINTS
Hellebores will wilt very quickly unless their stems are blanched. Put a medium saucepan of water on to boil. Cut each hellebore stem to the length you require and dip the end – about 3cm (1¹/₂in) – into the boiling water. Hold it there for about ten seconds until it is sealed.

1 Ensure your glass vases are completely clean. Wash the gravel to make sure it isn't muddy and place a small amount in the bottom of each vase. Fill them with water up to about two thirds full.

2 Cut some contorted willow for each vase. Treat the three vases as one arrangement, placing each branch so that the willow appears to drift as it might be dragged along the river. Let the willow hang to the front as well as to the sides so that the arrangement has depth from front to back.

3 Add the first type of hellebore (this is *H. orientalis*, the Lenten rose) to each vase, anchoring the stems by pushing them into the gravel. Keep the 'flow' of the arrangement in mind as you work, so that the direction of the hellebores goes with that of the willow.

4 Finally, add the other flowers. Here, other sorts of hellebores have been used and a few heads of creamy-flowered viburnum. These should fill out the body of the arrangement but not muddle the clean lines of the stems in the vases or obscure the overall shape created by the willow.

In the sunshine and open spaces of summer meadows, grasses rustle in the breeze and numerous varieties of flowers grow in colourful drifts among them. Field daisies, buttercups, poppies, gentians, cornflowers, cow parsley and yellow ranunculus grow among the grasses and bring to mind romantic bunches of flowers, tied together with raffia. In fact the origins of the wedding bouquet reside here. Traditionally the groom would go out and collect his bride's flowers in the morning and present them to her just before the wedding.

When purchasing cut flowers to recreate the feel of the meadow you are mostly looking for the small, star-like flowers that fall into the category of fillers. Cow parsley, saxifrage, bluebells and cornflowers are good examples, while the round marguerites and gentians are the jewels in your arrangements.

THE MEADOW

Alpine Meadow Bowl

YOU WILL NEED
ceramic bowl
black plastic sheeting or bin liner
florist's bowl to fit inside ceramic bowl
chicken wire
dried grasses
marguerite daisies
buttercups
snakeshead fritillaries (*F. meleagris*)
forget-me-nots
bluebells
saxifrage
cow parsley

Summertime is the season that inspires you to use the entire colour palette. Just as they might be found in an alpine meadow, small clusters of many different flowers are threaded through the grasses at all different heights in an unrestrained mass of colour. This arrangement is designed so that as you look into it, the effect is one of wandering through a meadow in high summer, discovering new varieties and colours as you go.

PRACTICAL POINTS
This ceramic bowl was about 45cm (18in) in diameter. It took 4–5 bunches of grass and 2–3 bunches of mixed flowers. The possible choice of flowers is huge – anything in season that does not look too cultivated – but you should aim for a good variety and about the same number of each.

1 Ceramic bowls often have holes in the base, so line the bowl with black plastic before placing the florist's bowl inside it; this will prevent water leaking on to the furniture.

2 Make a ball of chicken wire to fill the bowl and hold it in place with reel wire. Tie a ring of reel wire around the bowl just under the rim and secure the chicken wire to it at four equally spaced points with short lengths of reel wire. Tuck the ends out of sight. Fill the bowl with water.

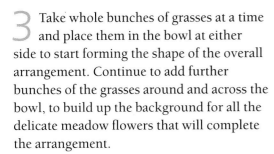

3 Take whole bunches of grasses at a time and place them in the bowl at either side to start forming the shape of the overall arrangement. Continue to add further bunches of the grasses around and across the bowl, to build up the background for all the delicate meadow flowers that will complete the arrangement.

4 Now start to add the flowers, keeping them in groups, just as they would be found growing. Vary the heights, too – here the marguerite daisies are low among the grass stems and the buttercups drift through them slightly higher up.

5 Forget-me-nots added in places around the edge of the bowl are allowed to overhang slightly and soften the line of the rim. A few fritillaries, angled to appear as though they are growing among the grasses, are added for a variation in shape and patterning.

6 Bluebells are added among the grass and other flowers, again hanging down slightly to further disguise the edge of the bowl. To make it more colourful, small pots of alpine plants – in their pots if your bowl is large enough – can be tucked in among the other flowers.

7 Finally, the arrangement is highlighted with several stems of cow parsley.

• THE MEADOW

Daisies in Meadow Grass

YOU WILL NEED
terracotta flower pot
reel wire
compost
moss
green raffia
bunches of wild grasses
potted plants of marguerites
    (*Argyranthemum frutescens*)

Out in the English countryside, summertime is synonymous with the wild flowers that line the roadsides and cover the fields with extravagant swathes of colour. Cornfields are stained red with poppies, while buttercups and daisies turn pastures from green to gold and white. It is this essence of summer meadows that has been caught in this simple but effective combination of daisies and ripening grasses.

PRACTICAL POINTS
You will need enough grass to cover the container without leaving any gaps – it may help to take the container with you when buying the grass to judge stem length and amount. This arrangement, in a pot about 45cm (18in) wide used 5 hand-sized bunches of grasses and 5 young marguerite plants. This could be easily scaled down, or even made with a small vase holding cut daisies in water.

1 Prepare the grasses by cutting them to approximately two and a half times the height of the container. Lay them down so that the bases of the stalks are in line, allowing some variation in height at the top.

2 Lay the container on the grasses and begin to wrap the reel wire around the grass and the container to hold them together. This is easier to do with some help or if you let the base of the container overhang the edge of the table or work top.

3 Once the first section is held securely with the reel wire, repeat step 2 until the whole container has a covering of grasses, bound a little above the base. Trim all the stalks level with the base of the container so that it can stand flat on the table.

4 Fill the container with fresh compost to
within approximately 5cm (2in) of the
rim. Take the marguerite plants out of their
pots at this stage and shake out the roots a
little. They will be planted in the container,
so this arrangement will last longer than
cut flowers.

5 Plant the marguerites in the container,
spacing them out as much as possible.
Tease out the flower stems, letting the flowers
and foliage show through and above the
grasses. Finally, take several strands of green
raffia and tie them around the container to
conceal the wire.

The most striking impressions of the beach are the wide stretches of monotone colours, where the sky meets the expanse of water and pale tones of blue-green and grey merge with muted tones of sand and pebbles at the shoreline.

Although not typically associated with flowers and foliage, the beach is a rich, natural source of inspiration for design, in terms of both colours and shapes. Shells and driftwood, starfish and seaweed, even rope and fishermen's netting, all provide the ingredients for beautiful decorations. It is the combined effects of bleached out and chalky colours – along with the shapes of starfish and twisted driftwood – that define these arrangements.

THE BEACH

Seashells and Candles

To evoke the pale, bleached colours of a stony beach, this table decoration is based on a collection of shells and pebbles in a circular arrangement of candles. The stronger shapes of starfish and larger shells provide the body of the arrangement, with moss and seaweed as fillers. The pale terracotta of the starfish and the darker stones create a muted contrast with the auricula flowers that have been chosen for their subtle colours.

YOU WILL NEED

plastic dish
2 blocks of floral foam (pre-soaked: see page 22)
candles
florist's sticks
stones and pebbles
selection of shells, chosen for their interesting
    shapes and colours
seaweed
starfish
pots of pale-coloured auriculas or primulas
gardenias
dried moss, to fill gaps

PRACTICAL POINTS

Starfish, driftwood and shells can all be bought from specialist shops (some species of seashell are now protected, so do ensure the ones you buy are appropriately harvested). You can buy stones and shells with ready-made holes through them, or drill small holes through the shells with a very fine masonry bit at a slow speed. This 5-candle centrepiece used about 40 shells in various sizes, 4 starfish and 8 pots of auriculas.

This arrangement is designed to be made on site at the table. If you wanted to move it, you would have to secure and wire the stones and shells in place or make it on a tray.

If not using candle holders, put sticky tape over the base and bottom 2cm (1in) of the candles. When the candles are pushed into the wet floral foam this will prevent them from soaking water up into the wick.

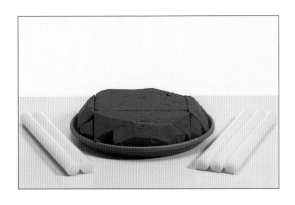

1 Fill the dish with floral foam, using offcuts from the main blocks to fit. Slope the sides off at a slight angle using a kitchen knife, so that the overall shape is slightly rounded off.

2 Place the candles in a ring on the floral foam (as widely spaced as possible) either using special candle holders or simply covering the ends with sticky tape (see page 52) and pressing them into the floral foam. Push a florist's stick up through a hole in the base of each auricula pot.

3 Add the auriculas, pushing the pots on their sticks into the floral foam at intervals all the way around and over the top of the arrangement.

4 Begin to build up heaps of pebbles and stones around and through the arrangement. Wherever you can, use them to screen the auricula pots. Ensure they are not too precariously balanced or the whole structure may tumble once the shells and other items are added.

Continue to build up the arrangement with your collection of shells, putting them where they will stay in place and be shown off to best advantage. Use as great a variety of shapes and textures as you can, and display some to show their mother-of-pearl interiors.

6 Some starfish have been added here for their slightly stronger terracotta colour, echoed by the auricula flowers. Spaces can be filled with seaweed or even pale moss, attached with stub pins. This will help to disguise the edges of pots and fill out the body of the arrangement. Leave space for some fresh flowers if you like.

7 Gardenias inserted among the shells keep the theme of pale, shoreline colours. Their strong white petals are reminiscent of shells and they soften any of the harder lines in the arrangement. Clean the leaves off the stems and push them carefully into the floral foam at different heights.

Beach Wall Garland

YOU WILL NEED
chicken wire
sack (sphagnum) moss for pad
black plastic sheeting or bin liner
stub wires
galvanized wire
driftwood or other suitable wood
shells, starfish etc. with holes in them
old rope
stones with holes in them
vials for individual flowers
'Casablanca' lilies
shaggy moss, lichen or dried seaweed,
   to fill gaps

Wall garlands are almost invariably designed as you go along, evolving naturally from your collection of artefacts. This one is inspired by the sea, taking its overall shape from branches of driftwood and the rope threaded through its length.

Dry arrangements such as this will last almost indefinitely, but for a special occasion fresh flowers can be added. Lilies or gardenias, which have the same iridescent quality as shells, are the perfect complement to this garland.

PRACTICAL POINTS

The possibilities for a garland like this are infinite, as a particularly interesting piece of driftwood might inspire a quite different approach – the list above is what was used here. As well as rope, you can use fishing net or different fabrics to help add movement. For a garland this size, about 75cm (2½ft) long, you will need about 3–4 'antlers' of driftwood and about three dozen shells in assorted sizes.

To make a hanging loop for a garland, cut a length of galvanized wire and twist the ends through the top end of the moss pad, leaving a loop long enough to hang the garland. Check it is fastened securely enough to take the weight of the whole wall hanging.

1 To make the pad for the garland cut a
  length of chicken wire about 30cm (12in)
less than the intended finished length (the
driftwood will exceed the frame) and twice
the width. Fold it in half and stuff moss
between the two layers to form a sandwich
of moss. Secure the open sides by twisting
the loose ends of cut wire together.

2 Cut a strip of plastic about 8cm (3in)
  larger than the pad on all sides.
Fold several stub wires in half to form pins
(see picture). Tucking the edges of the
plastic under, fix it to the back of the pad
with the pins.

3 All the elements of the design will need
  to have stub wire ties before they can
be attached to the frame. There is an element
of trial and error here as the exact position of
the wire will depend on the size and shape
of the item and where you want to position it.
The shells have been drilled so that they can
be wired in place (see page 52).

4 Begin with the driftwood branches that define the outline of the whole garland. Each piece is placed at a different height, creating the overall feeling of branches growing out of the garland. Bear in mind that a wall hanging should taper a little, with the top slightly wider than the bottom.

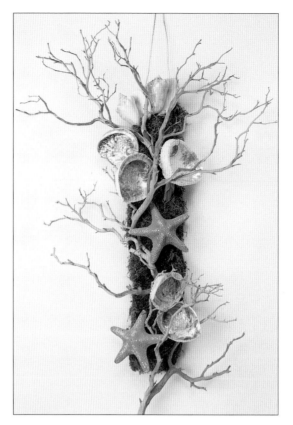

5 Attach the larger shells and starfish in place by pushing their wires right through the pad and bending them at the back. Make sure each item is quite secure. It may be necessary to push a wire back through to the front of the frame to do this, but this will be covered up at the end.

6 Continue to add smaller shells and starfish, as well as some pieces of flat driftwood. Offer each one up to the arrangement in order to see how it will work best. It is quite important to stand back frequently and make sure that the overall design is balanced and no lines are too straight or symmetrical.

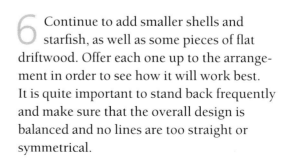

7 Weave in the rope next, so that some of it will be hidden and it won't all sit on top of the finished garland. Hold it in place with stub wires at various points, pushing them right through the pad to the back. Fix it at the top first and then trail it down, looping it as you go – imagine the flow of water, which would naturally follow the path of least resistance around the shells and driftwood and aim to take the rope in a flowing line down through the arrangement.

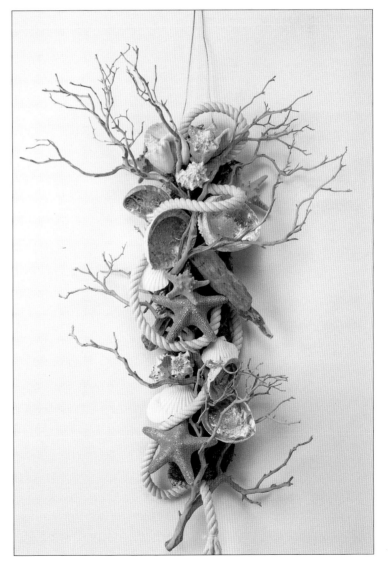

8 You can now add all the remaining shells and wire in any pebbles and small starfish. Fill any gaps with moss, lichen or strands of seaweed. Disguise the hanging wire with a length of thin rope, raffia or rough-textured string.

9 As a final embellishment, fresh 'Casablanca' lilies and lichen have been added. These particular lilies have almost shell-like petals and their shape imitates that of starfish so they are the ideal finishing touch. Cut each stem quite short and insert it into a water vial. Push the vial into the arrangement so it is held in place. They can go at an angle – even partly behind shells or starfish to add depth to the garland.

Remove pollen from lilies wherever possible as soon as the flower opens as it can stain. Once a flower has opened, place your fingers and thumb very gently around the base of the stamen and pull them the length of the anthers so that the pollen sacs come off in your hand. If pollen dust does get on to clothes, do not disturb it until you can lift it off with a strip of sticky tape.

INSPIRATION

The Topiary Garden
❧

TOPIARY WITH TULIPS

The Herbaceous Border
❧

COTTAGE GARDEN BASKET

The Kitchen Garden
❧

HARVEST RING

MOSS URN WITH APPLES

MAJESTIC SUMMER URN

HAND-TIED HERBS

FROM THE GARDEN

The Potting Shed

WALL TROPHY

FLOWERING SEED TRAY

The Orchard

CHERRY BLOSSOM BASKET

AUTUMN APPLE BASKET

The Conservatory

PLANTED JASMINE AND GARDENIAS

LEAF VASE WITH GLORIOSA LILIES

If you consider the topiary garden as a source of inspiration your thoughts might turn to images of precisely shaped hedges, from simple box borders to elaborately clipped, sculptured shapes and intricately designed mazes.

A close look, however, will take you beyond the sculpted animals and the complexities of the maze to the traditional topiary knot garden in which small hedges were grown in symmetrical patterns. Flowers or herbs were planted so that they filled the topiary shapes. Often each shape in the pattern surrounded one type of flower so that the effect was single, confined blocks of colour which formed part of an overall design. Frequently these shaped hedges were used to separate the different herbs in a herb garden, each one completely enclosed in its own circle or pattern of topiary.

plastic florist's bowl
chicken wire
reel wire
scissors
bushy stems of box foliage
tulips

PRACTICAL POINTS
This arrangement was made in a large florist's
bowl nearly 30 cm (12 in) across and needed
8 bunches of tulips. It would easily be repro-
duced using a smaller bowl and 3–4 bunches
of tulips or other suitable flowers in season.
Be aware that the nature of tulips is such that
no matter how carefully you arrange them,
they will grow towards the light. This bowl
could also be planted with herbs, as these were
also grown in the traditional topiary garden.

Topiary
with Tulips

The close-cut precision of the green foliage is a
wonderful complement to these flame-coloured
tulips. By covering a container with box leaves and
clipping it neatly into shape you can recreate a
dense topiary border to be filled with the flowers
of your choice. For a dramatic effect select a single
variety of strongly shaped flowers, such as these
'Rococo' tulips. For a more romantic feel a mixture
of roses could spill gently over the topiary bowl.

Although box trimmings are suggested
here, a good alternative is curly cupressus,
a springy type of conifer which will also clip well
into shape. It is available from many florists.

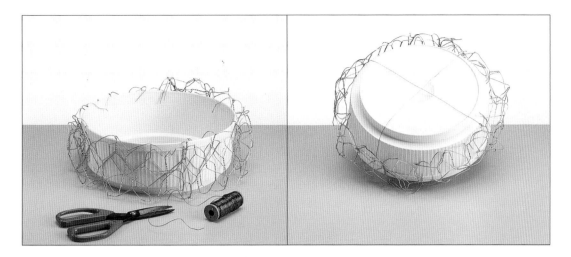

1 Take a piece of chicken wire roughly three times the depth of the bowl and long enough to go around it and overlap slightly. Form it into a roll of three layers, flattening it as you bend it around the bowl and, where the ends of the roll meet, twist stray wires together to hold it. Bend the overlap over the top of the bowl to help keep it in place. To prevent the chicken wire from lifting off, stretch two strands of reel wire across the underneath of the bowl, twisting the ends into the chicken wire to secure it.

2 Cut box sprigs 10–15cm (4–6in) long and push them firmly into the chicken wire. Start with vertical sprigs, then create a bushy mass of sprigs at all different angles, to resemble an uncut hedge.

3 Carefully clip the box with scissors, paying particular attention to the angle of the top and the sides which should be as near to a perfect right angle as possible. It will help if you hold the scissors level against the foliage as you clip.

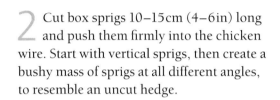

4 Make a ball of chicken wire to fill the
   bowl, so that the top of the mound rises
just above the rim. Fill the bowl with water.

5 Cut the tulips to the required height,
   making sure that they are all the
same length. Insert the flowers a few at a
time, working across the bowl in different
directions and then filling in the gaps.

Moss Urn
with Apples

Topiary is an example of the gardener's skilled control over natural forms. This apple urn echoes the formality of these clipped designs with its strong, clean outline and classical style. The bold single colour is a reminder of a Victorian dinner party, where a banqueting table would be laden with elegant pyramids of fresh fruit. Lemons or oranges would work equally well.

PRACTICAL POINTS
It is important to give the pyramid a stable base, ensuring it is weighted down before you start to build the chicken wire frame. If possible make it *in situ* so there is no need to move it afterwards. This urn, standing almost 1m (3ft) high, took about 70 apples, but the idea could be adapted to a table decoration, using a small urn and proportionally smaller fruit, such as clementines.

1 Make sure the moss is clean – you may need to pick out leaves, twigs and pine needles. To cover the urn, take flat pieces of moss in sections as large as possible to minimize the number of joins. Glue them directly on to the urn with the glue gun, piecing them together like a jigsaw.

2 Once the whole of the outside of the urn is covered, including the rim, stand back and check for gaps. Trim any stray pieces of moss to emphasize the clean silhouette, then spray it with green paint to make it last.

3 Pack the gravel or bricks into the urn to counterbalance the weight of the apples. Scrunch up the chicken wire tightly into a tall dome, so it will hold its shape and support the fruit. Attach to the urn with reel wire (see page 43). Poke sack moss into the wire frame to block the light and add anchorage for the apples.

4 Once the chicken wire framework is filled with sack moss, begin to wire on the apples. Thread a stub wire through each apple, twisting the ends together at the stalk, so that when the wires are threaded into the chicken wire frame the apples are all facing the same way. Build the pyramid up in rings from the base, so you are not left with large awkward gaps, but do not try to regiment the apples too much.

5 Before you wire on the top section of apples, add the spider plant. Take the plant out of its pot, shake off any loose soil and wrap the roots in black plastic. Cut a hole in the top of the chicken wire frame and slot in the plant, pressing the chicken wire back into shape around it.

6 Continue to cover the frame with apples. Fill in the small gaps between the apples with flat moss – just push it in with your finger, as the apples will hold the moss in place.

The herbaceous border is synonymous with the English country garden. While the pretty cottage garden was typically chaotic, the long herbaceous borders of grand country houses had a colourful but more regulated style.

By its nature, the herbaceous border is cut right back over the winter and grows up from the ground each year into a riot of colour. Strictly, it does not include shrubs and is characterized by the juxtaposition of the shapes and colours. Delphiniums, foxgloves and grand ornamental artichokes grow in bold drifts above peonies and campanulas. Phloxes in brilliant shades contrast with the greens of euphorbias, hostas and alchemilla. While the herbaceous border can inspire on a much grander scale, there is a similar quality to the meadow arrangements in that the flowers and ornamental foliage grow in drifts among each other.

The two designs in this chapter encapsulate both the grandeur and informal style of the traditional border. Like many modern herbaceous borders, they include shrubs to give a framework to the designs.

Cottage Garden Basket

There are two important contrasts in the herbaceous border – the different colours of the flowers and the variety of shapes of flower stems and foliage. Reflecting this, white peonies and blue campanula bells are set against the tall spires of foxgloves and irises. Alchemilla and astilbe grow between the taller flowers. To retain the sense of depth of the herbaceous border, flowers are arranged in groups rather than singly, with space around them so that you can see through and among the flowers and foliage.

YOU WILL NEED

suitable basket, quite large
black plastic sheeting or bin liner
bucket to fit inside the basket
scrap paper, newspaper, cardboard or
    polystyrene
sack (sphagnum) moss
chicken wire
reel wire
sticks for the daisy pots (1 x 10cm long)
branches of guelder rose (*Viburnum opulus*)
large-headed euphorbia such as *E. wulfenii*
crown imperials (*Fritillaria imperialis*)
aquilegia
alchemilla
astilbes
long-stemmed campanulas
foxgloves
phloxes
Canterbury bells (*Campanula media*)
white peonies
irises

PRACTICAL POINTS

To create this style of decoration on any scale, choose whatever flowers are available locally, and in season. Look for shapes to create the contrasts achieved here. A large basket like this will need something approaching 100 stems, with 10–12 varieties to give the right balance. A smaller version would not include as many varieties, so reduce the number of different types of flower rather than the number of stems of each, keeping the balance of spikes, rounded shapes and fillers.

To make euphorbias last, singe the cut end of the stem to seal in the white sap. Avoid the sap as it can be an irritant.

1 Line a large basket with black plastic to prevent the arrangement from leaking on to the furniture and also to stop light shining through the basket weave. Place the bucket into the centre of the basket and pack out the gap between with crumpled newspaper or whatever you have available to hold the bucket steady. Disguise the packing with a topping of sack moss, tucking in the moss so that it won't dip in the water – otherwise it will siphon the water into the basket.

2 Make a ball of chicken wire to fill the bucket and hold this in place at four equally spaced points with reel wire. Thread it through the basket and back through the chicken wire, twisting the ends together to hold the chicken wire securely. Tuck the ends out of sight. Fill the bucket with water.

3 Begin with the euphorbia and guelder rose, to establish the overall shape. These provide the core foliage and the greenery through which the flower colours can appear to drift, as they would in the border.

4 Working with the spiky shapes to start with, insert the fritillaries as a group, followed by the aquilegia. Use some bushy heads of alchemilla to fill out the front of the arrangement.

5 Begin to fill in the spaces. Position the astilbes so that they froth out towards the front of the arrangement and add a mass of campanulas above them, sitting among the fritillaries and aquilegias.

6 Add foxgloves, in a group to balance with the height of the fritillaries, and taller fillers, phloxes and Canterbury bells, to drift through the arrangement as if they were growing among the other flowers.

7 A touch of drama is added to the arrangement with the strong round shapes of the white peonies and the irises. Placed centrally, the peonies provide a focal point to the whole decoration, while irises are seen at their best in silhouette.

Majestic Summer Urn

This is an arrangement on the grand scale, to display the many different varieties of flowers found in the herbaceous border at its best. Delphiniums, foxgloves and giant alliums are used at full length, with large heads of hydrangeas and long trails of roses to bring the full glory of the summer garden into the decoration. The finished pedestal arrangement, which measured nearly 3m (9ft) tall, is a splendid way to decorate a church or create a grand entrance for a special occasion.

YOU WILL NEED
stone garden urn with pedestal
galvanized metal bucket
chicken wire
bamboo canes
thin galvanized wire
reel wire
sack (sphagnum) moss
stub wire
extension tubes
branches of beech and forsythia
long branches of 'New Dawn' climbing rose
potted variegated ivy
foxtails (*Eremurus robustus*)
agapanthus
delphiniums
giant alliums (flowering onions)
potted hydrangeas
alchemilla
foxgloves
echinops
monkshood (*Aconitum napellus*)
white peonies
'Hollywood' roses

PRACTICAL POINTS
Despite its size, about the same number of flowers were used as in the Cottage Basket (see page 76), but the long branches of foliage and and climbing rose create the large framework.

Single extension tubes (see page 16) are attached with florist's tape to bamboo sticks to extend the height of flowers and to fit in small bunches that won't go into the chicken wire or reach the water.

1 Fold and pleat enough chicken wire to fill the bucket. Use a bamboo cane to push it right down into the bucket, then tease it up so it stands high above the rim. Pack the chicken wire well – too little will not hold the stems securely and, scrunched together too tightly, it will not allow you to push the stems down into the bucket. Check you can push a cane right down through the wire and it is held in place. Secure the chicken wire with lengths of reel wire and a ring of galvanized wire under the rim of the urn (see page 43). Conceal the wire with moss, pushing it into the chicken wire, and fill the bucket with water.

2 The foliage creates the overall shape. As this is a front-facing arrangement, keep the foliage towards the back of the container – you need to leave plenty of space in front for the flowers or they will be lost among the foliage. The branches should create a backdrop that is not too dense or heavy looking.

3 Add the trailing material next, to bring the pedestal into the arrangement. Push the long branches of climbing roses well down into the chicken wire. The ivies are kept in their pots, so insert a stub wire through the base of each pot and attach it to the chicken wire. Check the trails are falling in a natural-looking way and add a little foliage at the side to fill out the silhouette.

4 Next, the spiky shapes – foxtails, agapanthuses and delphiniums – are added. These will define the height limit of the arrangement, so use the extension tubes as required, and keep these tall stems in groups rather than dotting them singly around the arrangement.

5 For an arrangement on this scale the round shapes need to be large and impressive. Rather than individual hydrangea heads, use the entire plants, still in their pots – push a short bamboo cane through the base of each pot to extend them and make them easier to secure, and place the canes directly into the chicken wire. Add the giant alliums, too, at this stage.

6 Use alchemilla in drifts through the heart of the arrangement as a filler. It will be eventually partly hidden, but provides depth to the finished arrangement. The smaller globes of the echinops and shorter spikes of foxgloves and monkshood are also used now, to help fill out the display.

7 In this last stage the highlights are added in the form of open peonies and roses. These are placed in small bunches around the centre of the display so that they emerge from among the alchemilla. They should be presented as they grow in the herbaceous border, so avoid placing them singly or filling up every space.

A Victorian country house depended on its kitchen garden. Fresh vegetables were required all year round to feed what were often large house parties and the lady of the house would expect to have her favourite flowers available to decorate the halls, even out of season. Magnificent floral displays for the table and the large public rooms were traditionally arranged by the head gardener, who was a key member of the staff and had often been in training from apprenticeship as a youth. Managing the kitchen garden was as much an art as a craft and he would have at his finger tips clever techniques to grow fruit out of season and force special vegetables and flowers.

Today, a kitchen garden is a much smaller and rarer sight, but vegetables, fruit and herbs are as rich a source of inspiration for indoor displays as flowers from the decorative parts of the garden.

Harvest Ring

YOU WILL NEED
floral foam wreath (pre-soaked: see page 22)
stub wires
bunches of carrots with stalks attached
baby pumpkins
ornamental kale
asparagus spears
small red cabbages
garlic
red onions
rue
'Little Silver' spray roses
lichen or reindeer moss

For the candle holders
small terracotta pots
church candles
strong elastic bands
raffia or decorative cord
leaves from a Savoy cabbage

The kitchen garden provides a dynamic display, vibrant with colour. Ornamental kale, turning gently from green to deep purple in the centre reflects the deep red of the onions and is complemented by the orange of the pumpkins and carrots. Here, the straight, spiky shapes are the carrots and asparagus spears and the body of the arrangement comes from the solid round shapes of onions, garlic bulbs, cabbages and pumpkins. The whole arrangement is brought together with softly toned roses.

PRACTICAL POINTS
Forming the basis of this 40cm (16in) ring were 2 large bunches of carrots, 4 baby pumpkins, 3 ornamental kale and 2 bunches of asparagus, with 2 bunches of spray roses. Choose whatever is in season – miniature vegetables work particularly well in a smaller ring.

1 Tightly wire several different vegetables by twisting or threading the full stub wire and folding it in half so that a hair-pin style stem of wire is left sticking out. For carrots you can wire the stalks together and then cut off the foliage, so they can hang off the wreath in a bunch. For asparagus, wrap the wire around the middle of several spears, allowing them to cross slightly. Stab a wire through the stalk part of the onions, cabbages, pumpkin and garlic bulbs.

2 There is an overall movement to the arrangement and the carrots and asparagus spears will create the direction of that movement. Attach the carrots first, spacing the bunches around the wreath and angling them to give a feel of rotation in one direction. The pumpkins are added here to mark the three main focal points of the circle, around which the other vegetables will cluster. In all cases the wire pins are pressed straight into the floral foam wreath.

3 Add the asparagus spears, positioning them to follow the direction of rotation. Ornamental kale and little cabbages introduce the green and purple colours in this scheme and are placed to build up the three groups around the pumpkins. (The red cabbages are sliced in half to show their lovely marbled interior; if they won't lie flat, slice the backs off with a knife.)

4 The roses are are an important part of the arrangement and need a certain amount of space to work in, so these should be added next. Group them in sprays around the pumpkin/cabbage focal points – singly or in meagre clusters they will be overpowered by the strong shapes and colours of the vegetables.

5 Fill out the spaces that remain with smaller vegetables: red onions to deepen the purple colours and garlic to mimic the shape of the rosebuds. Remember to keep moving around the wreath to check that there are no noticeable gaps or imbalances from any angle. Tuck sprigs of rue into some of the remaining spaces; it will also serve to soften the silhouettes of the vegetables and add depth of colour to the pale roses. Fill any small remaining holes with little pieces of lichen or reindeer moss. Moss or raffia can also cover any scraps of wiring still visible.

6 To make the accompanying candle holders, select two clean Savoy cabbage leaves of similar size for each terracotta pot. Wrap them round the pot from opposite sides and where they overlap secure with an elastic band. Trim the base of the cabbage leaves so that the pot can stand properly. Tie a few strands of raffia over the elastic band to hide it and fill the overlap with a tiny sprig of lichen moss. Secure each candle in its pot by melting the candle's base slightly.

Hand-tied
Herbs

YOU WILL NEED
raffia
flat-leaf parsley
dill in flower
marjoram
rosemary
sage
dried lavender
calendula or common marigold

This tied bunch is made using herbs straight from the kitchen garden. If the dining room is to be set to delight the senses, then such simple bouquets tied to some of the chairs will look lovely and fill the room with the fragrant aroma of lavender and rosemary. The soft grey-green colouring of the rosemary branches provides a useful starting point for any herb bouquet, but after that your own taste and colour scheme can dictate any number of different combinations.

PRACTICAL POINTS
As well as being attached to a chairback as an unusual presentation, this tied bunch can readily be placed in a vase as a table centrepiece. Similar bunches, but scaled down, can be made from tiny stems of herbs and a few flowers to decorate individual place settings.

When constructing any hand-tied bunch, remember to support all the stems but not to hold them so tightly that it is difficult to slide in new stems.

1 To keep the lower part of the stems as light as possible, strip the leaves and flowers downwards from the point where the stems will cross and be bound together – roughly half way down. Divide the herbs into small bunches of each type and lay them out ready to be used. Wire together small bundles of lavender with stub wire, leaving a length of wire like a single long stem.

2 Gather up three stems of rosemary to create the central body of the arrangement. Hold them loosely and let them fall into a spray. Hold the next stem across the junction of the first three, turning the arrangement slowly round in a spiralling motion as you add stems.

3 Place the herbs in small bunches, not single stems, so that each type shows up clearly. Spiral the growing bouquet around in your hand as you add sprays of marjoram, sage, dill, flat-leaf parsley and so on.

4 When adding the bunches of lavender, the 'stem extension' of stub wire (see Step 1) allows you to insert the bundles easily without adding greatly to the number of stems in your hand.

5 Here the marigolds have been placed to separate the blocks of lavender colour. Thread them into the edges and centre of the arrangement so they are not all at the same height. They are deliberately placed unevenly and slightly to one side, just as they might grow. As you turn the bunch around in your hand, check for gaps and add a few stems of dill or flat-leaf parsley around the outside.

6 To finish off, a few more flowers are added so that the arrangement tends to dip rather than dome slightly at the centre – when the arrangement is *in situ* you will have a quite different view of it than when you are holding it in your hand. When the bouquet is complete, bind it round with raffia and tie it off, cutting the stems all to the same length, about 15–20cm (6–8in).

7 Tie several strands of raffia in a bow and attach it to the bunch, cutting the tails just short of the stems. Tease out the raffia strands to give the bow extra fullness.

The potting shed might at first seem an unusual place to find inspiration. An initial glance may not trigger the imagination as readily as a colourful meadow or a bright summer garden. But, unearth a forgotten trug or ornamental seed tray and they can be used with a few clay pots to make a pretty and simple planted arrangement.

For something more elaborate, the humble potting shed can become an excellent source of artefacts, with pots and tools forming part of an unusual and dramatic wall decoration. There was a time when every aristocratic family displayed its shield or coat of arms as part of a wall trophy, along with swags of fabric, bunches of wheat, scythes and farming tools, even spears and guns. Heraldic wall trophies are still to be seen in the magnificent wood-carvings of Grinling Gibbons or the plasterwork stucco in an Adam interior.

Like heraldic painting, this kind of decoration is an art form that has been extended in recent years. It was Kenneth Turner, the celebrated London florist, who first put together the idea of using garden tools, flowers and plants to recreate floral decorations as elaborate wall trophies.

chicken wire
sack (sphagnum) moss for pad
bamboo canes
small saw to trim the bamboo
black plastic sheeting or bin liner
stub wires
galvanized wire
green flat moss to hide chicken wire
tools such as trowels, forks, watering can,
    shears etc.
equipment such as a trug, sieve, flower pots etc.
raffia
wheat
pots of heather plants
pots of trailing ivy
pots or trays of pansies

Wall Trophy

Wall trophies and garlands make a dramatic
statement. Hung like a painting, a trophy such as
this can reflect the seasons if you replace the plants
and flowers according to the time of year. At
Christmas time, for example, holly and ivy, fruits,
nuts and berries, and even swags of tartan fabric
can be incorporated to give it a festive air.

PRACTICAL POINTS

No two wall trophies are likely to be the same.
These steps are designed to show you how
to make a base and gradually build the
arrangement, letting your design evolve
naturally from the collection of pieces and
the plants you have chosen. It helps to lay out
the components on the ground first and try
out possible permutations, so you have an idea
of where different pieces might best fit.
This will also indicate the size of pad you will
need to make. This finished trophy measures
about 90 x 60cm (3 x 2ft).

1 To make a flat base pad, cut a piece of chicken wire twice the size of the pad you will need. Fold it in half and stuff moss into the sandwich to form a thick, flat pad. Secure the pad by twisting the loose ends of cut wire together. Cut two canes slightly larger than the diagonal and push them through the middle of the moss from corner to corner, forming a cross. This is to stop the pad from flexing.

2 Trim the bamboo with a small saw so that the ends only just extend from the corners of the pad. Cut a sheet of plastic about 8cm (3in) larger than the pad on all sides. Fold several stub wires in half to form pins (see picture). Tucking the edges of the plastic under, fix it to the back of the pad with the pins. Make a hanging loop of galvanized wire attached firmly to the two top corners of the pad. Twist the wire ends right through the moss and chicken wire from one side to the other, testing it will take the weight.

3 All the elements of the design you want to attach to the pad will need to be wired. This shows you how to wire various objects including a trug, garden fork, flower pot and wheatsheaf. The exact position of the wire will depend on the size and shape of the item and where you want to position it.

4 Hold up the first items, the wheat and the sieve, to the pad to determine where they will be placed. As the chicken wire will show through the sieve, hide it with green moss pinned to the pad using stub wire (cut to about 10cm/8in) bent into pins. Wire the wheat into hand-sized bunches and attach them to the pad to form a dense spray. The edges of the plaque tend to be the most vulnerable, so poke the wire right through the pad and wrap it over the edge for extra strength.

5 To attach heavy items like the sieve and the watering can it is not enough to twist the stub pins around the chicken wire base – the pins need to go right through the pad and have their ends twisted tightly together at the back. To make sure the sieve stayed securely in place, additional wires were twisted as inconspicuously as possible around the sieve grid and the chicken wire behind it. The watering can was wired to the sieve, then its spout was firmly attached to the pad. It may require some help to hold these larger pieces while they are being fastened.

6 Offer up some of the other items to the
arrangement, deciding where they will
help create depth and balance. At this stage
do not worry if wires show as the flowers and
foliage will hide them. It is more important
to ensure that the objects are securely fixed
exactly where you want them to go – here
the basket is wired in several places and the
bamboo is attached to the sieve and the can
wherever the wires will hold securely.

7 To complete the structure of the wall
trophy, shears have been pushed in
underneath the sieve and the scythe, which
is quite a strong shape, has been laid across
the wheat rather than used in isolation – this
creates an appropriate context for it and
avoids disturbing the overall shape of the
arrangement. Keep standing back to view the
silhouette. The long-handled trowel and fork
have been set here to balance the shears and
the small ones wired in place to associate
with the trug.

8 Once the trophy's structure is complete, the floral elements can be added. To attach the potted plants, push a wire into the hole in the base of the pot to emerge through the earth at the top, then bend it down and twist the two ends together. The pots can then be wired into place – here the heather gives colour and depth to the trophy and the ivy has been allowed to trail over the tools, to soften the silhouette.

9 Add moss to fill in the gaps and place the pansies in the trug, leaving the roots and soil showing. Raffia has been used to hide the wires around the middle of the bamboo canes and a length was twisted behind the watering can to leave its ends trailing under the ivy. Strands of ivy were twisted up part of the hanging wire as a finishing touch.

Flowering Seed Tray

Simple and rustic, this arrangement rediscovers the decorative possibilities in familiar and often overlooked items. Through the winter this easily made and long-lasting display will bring a touch of spring to a table or deep window sill, and with a few minutes' replanting become a pretty summer decoration later in the year.

YOU WILL NEED
trug
black plastic sheeting or bin liner
green moss
small earthenware flower pots
potting compost
Pots or tray of pansies
lichen or reindeer moss

PRACTICAL POINTS
It might take a bit of searching to find a lovely old wooden trug or seed tray. One like this is ideal, as it is very sturdy but attractive, and big enough to hold several flower pots on a flat base. Other seasonal suggestions might include: miniature spring bulbs such as *Iris reticulata*, seed-sown dwarf summer annuals or autumn crocuses.

1 Brush down the tray and terracotta pots to clean them, but without spoiling the natural weathering and signs of age that will contribute to the rustic appeal of this simple arrangement.

2 Line the tray with black plastic to ensure that water or residual damp will not leak from the arrangement. Bear in mind that moss can siphon water, so protect furniture accordingly.

3 To disguise the plastic, give the whole tray a lining of green moss. Because the design of this tray means the black plastic is also visible from the outside, more moss has been stuffed between the slats.

If you can't find an old trug or pots, then this arrangement could be given a more contemporary feel using a painted trug and new terracotta pots.

4 Remove the pansy plants from their seed
tray or plastic pots and plant them up
individually in fresh potting compost in the
earthenware pots.

5 Cover up the soil in each pot with little
pieces of lichen or reindeer moss tucked
under the pansy leaves. Simply place the filled
flower pots in the mossy tray. With regular
watering this arrangement should last well,
especially if kept in the best possible conditions for the type of plants you have chosen.
Keep it in good light as much as possible.

The orchard changes dramatically with each season. Winter branches bud into a foam of pink and white blossom, which is soon followed by the fresh green of the new spring leaves. As summer progresses, the fruits ripen, and the golds and russets of apples and pears give way to the richer colours of autumn. The orchard is perhaps at its finest in spring and autumn, and the arrangements in this chapter draw on these two seasons for inspiration.

In spring, early flowers cluster among the tree roots beneath the canopy of blossom, while in autumn the atmosphere is moodier, the colours richer and the branches are laden with ripening fruit. Both in baskets, these two designs can easily decorate a hall table or form a dining room centrepiece. On a different scale, using a number of smaller containers, they can bring the lightness of spring or the warmth of autumn into different corners of the home.

Cherry Blossom Basket

This basket captures the mood in the middle of spring, when branches are thick with blossom and everything has a fresh, green feel to it. Rather than contorting the branches to fit a preconceived shape, the natural growth has been allowed to dictate the shape of the display. The flowers used to fill out the arrangement complete the sense of an old orchard in full flower.

YOU WILL NEED
suitable basket, quite large
black plastic sheeting or bin liner
large bucket that fits inside the basket
scrap paper, newspaper or cardboard to pack
    between bucket and basket
sack (sphagnum) moss
chicken wire
reel wire
sticks for the daisy pots (1 x 10cm long)
double pink cherry blossom
double white cherry blossom
choisya
guelder rose (*Viburnum opulus*)
'Angélique' tulips
pots of marguerite daisies (*Argyranthemum
    frutescens*)

PRACTICAL POINTS

About half a dozen branches of blossom were used in this decoration; the actual dimensions will depend on the length of the branches and the proportions of your basket. If using long branches, you will need the strength and rigidity of a metal bucket – a plastic one might bend under the weight.

1 Line the basket with black plastic to prevent the arrangement from leaking on to any furniture when it is watered and also to stop light shining through the basket weave. Place the bucket into the centre of the basket and fill the gap with crumpled newspaper or chunks of polystyrene – whatever is available to keep the bucket in place so that it won't tilt when filled. Cover the top of the packing with sack moss to hide it. Be sure to tuck the moss in so that it won't dip in the water, otherwise it will siphon the water into the basket.

2 Make a ball of chicken wire to fill the bucket and hold it in place at four equally spaced points with reel wire (see page 16), threading the wire through the basket and back through the chicken wire and twisting the ends together to hold the chicken wire securely. Tuck the ends out of sight. Fill the bucket with water.

3 Place the blossom stems into the bucket, pushing them in so they are firmly held by the chicken wire. Let the natural shape of the branches determine the outline of the arrangement. The aim is to reproduce the dynamic quality of the blossom tree, when the branches overhang with the weight of the flowers. Use branches at different lengths to give a sense of depth and three dimensions.

4 Add the choisya and guelder rose in the centre of the arrangement, among the blossom branches. These fillers have not been left too tall as, although they are giving density to the arrangement, they should not spoil the natural, extended silhouette of the blossom stems. Try to leave the basket handle showing as a feature.

5 The tulips are then placed in groups among the other stems. Push sticks firmly up into a hole in the base of the pots of marguerites, so that they can be pushed into the arrangement – the chicken wire will keep them securely in place. When in position low among the other flowers they will look clumped – just as they might be found growing under the trees.

Autumn
Apple
Basket

YOU WILL NEED
suitable basket
black plastic sheeting or bin liner
florist's plastic bowl that fits inside the basket
reel wire
moss
chicken wire
stub wires
red apples
branches, with red apples still attached
    if possible
crab apples on their branches
'Leonardo' roses
flat moss

This basket arrangement is quite different from the spring one (see page 108) and brings together the fruit and colours of autumn. There is a feel of laden branches of autumn leaves and ripe apples, ready to fall. Late summer roses add softness to the silhouette and fill up the basket. The variety used here is 'Leonardo', a very beautiful and unusually coloured rose, its shades of terracotta emphasizing the warm autumnal tones.

PRACTICAL POINTS
This basket was approximately 60 x 30cm (2 x 1ft) and needed half a dozen branches of fruit and about a dozen roses. You could recreate the arrangement on a smaller scale, using branches of crab apples and small bunches of spray roses and varieties of smaller berries. For added security, the fruit can be wired to the branches (see below).

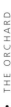 Some of these apples are fixed to the branch with wire. Wind a small piece of reel wire around the stalk, the other end around the branch to secure it.

1 Line the basket with black plastic or a bin liner to keep it waterproof and to prevent light from showing through the weave. Place the bowl in the middle of the basket and roughly trim the plastic to the edge of the basket. Stuff out the surround with moss to hide the plastic and fill the area around the bowl.

2 Make a ball of chicken wire and press it down to fill the bowl, teasing it back up above the rim. Thread lengths of reel wire through the chicken wire, attaching it to the basket at intervals all the way around, to hold the chicken wire securely in place. Fill the bowl with water.

3 To create the basic outline, take the sprays of crab apple and the apple branches. Keep a wide, open silhouette, using the branches to provide the spiky form and structure of the arrangement – take advantage of the natural shape that the branches grow in to guide you. Wire apples on to the branches with a short length of reel wire where they are needed – or are about to fall.

4 To fill in the arrangement and add body to the overall shape, place foliage, apples and roses at different depths. Keep them towards the centre and don't let them go above the height of the basket handle as if it is kept visible this can form part of the arrangement.

5 To make the basket itself densely packed, add more apples and roses – still at different heights to give the arrangement depth and a feeling of abundance. Some of the apples here have been wired in place to fix them.

6 Add flat moss around the edges and in the gaps and over the lip of the basket to hide any of the plastic. Take care not to let the moss touch the water as it will act as a siphon, soaking it up and dripping over the edge of the basket.

Many varieties of roses can be purchased without thorns, but if you do have thorned roses it is worth taking the time to remove them. Hold the base of the stem and cut the thorn tips with secateurs.

A conservatory immediately evokes images of light and sun shining through glass, an anticipation of warmth and the heady scents of hothouse flowers. There will be lush plants growing in a variety of flower pots and containers, and trails of climbing jasmine, bougainvillea, stephanotis and vines. Jungle-like foliage forms a backdrop to the elegant lines of such precious flowers as gardenias, orchids and lilies, all exuding their exotic perfumes.

Inspiration from the conservatory takes us from the bold leaves of the tiger plant to the delicate petals of jasmine and the rarer gloriosa lilies. The designs in this chapter are deliberately simple, allowing the dramatic colours and shapes of these tropical flowers and leaves to be shown to their full advantage.

Planted Jasmine and Gardenias

Although planted rather than arranged in water, this display is still treated as any other, with the shape evolving spontaneously from the contorted willow. The dark leaves of the gardenia form a natural foil for its creamy white flowers, which also contrast with the spirals of willow and trails of jasmine. The result is an elegant design that is full of exotic scents.

118

YOU WILL NEED
decorative terracotta pot
black plastic bag or bin liner
crocks (bits of broken flower pot, stones, gravel etc.)
potting compost
trailing jasmine
gardenias
contorted willow (*Salix tortuosa*), stripped of any leaves
moss

PRACTICAL POINTS
Most tropical plants need good conditions to grow well and gardenias are particularly fussy. They are sensitive to the chemicals in tap water, so for best results water them either with mineral water or distilled water.

1 The terracotta pot must be lined as it is
   porous. To do this lay the black plastic
bag inside the pot and trim it to roughly 5 cm
(2in) above the rim. A planted arrangement
needs drainage, so before adding the soil,
place a handful of old crocks in the bottom –
enough to loosely cover the base, taking care
not to pierce the plastic.

2 Give all the plants a good watering before
   taking them out of their growing pots.
Fill the terracotta pot half way with compost
and then carefully unwind the tendrils of
jasmine plants from their hoops.

3 Begin planting the container with a
   gardenia in the centre and the jasmines
to the edge, so the plants are well spread out.
Gently loosen the rootballs of each plant
and firm the compost around them without
compacting it too much.

4 Use a second gardenia to complete the planting. Press the soil well down and make sure the final surface is slightly below the height of the pot, or watering will cause it to overflow. Leave the jasmine trailing at this stage.

5 Place the contorted willow at intervals throughout the arrangement, pushing the branches into the soil around the edges and between the gardenia plants, so that the arrangement has depth and the willow branches don't just encircle the plants.

6 Thread the trailing lengths of jasmine along and across the willow branches. Without forcing the jasmine stems into shapes, let their natural tendency guide you as you pick them up, so that they appear to grow and twist naturally around the willow. They will form a soft, three-dimensional framework around the gardenias. As a final touch, fill the gaps between the gardenias and jasmine plants with moss, particularly around the edges of the pot.

Leaf Vase with Gloriosa Lilies

straight-sided glass vase
strong elastic bands
short length of old rope, raffia or tasselled cord,
   according to style
tiger leaves (*Maranta leuconeura*)
gloriosas (*Gloriosa superba*)

Tropical flowers, such as these gloriosa lilies, can be so stunning and intricate in their colours and shapes that they are often most successfully displayed on their own. Here the simplest of hand-made containers has been made with leaves from a maranta plant to complement the lilies. These dark, striped leaves, appropriately sometimes called tiger leaves, would make a fitting contrast to other exotic flowers such as birds of paradise (*Strelitzia*) and orchids.

PRACTICAL POINTS

This vase required 8 maranta leaves and contains 5 stems of gloriosa lilies. The idea could be extended to decorating a dinner table, by wrapping several small glasses in leaves and filling them with flowers – or indeed candles.

The way to ensure the longest possible vase life for cut flowers is to change the water regularly, replacing it with fresh water so the flowers can breathe the oxygen.

1 Choose a suitable straight-sided vase slightly shorter than the length of your maranta leaves – this arrangement is most effective if the leaves are taller than the container so it is completely hidden.

2 Wrap three of the leaves around the vase, placing one over the other so that they overlap quite closely. Hold them in place with one of the elastic bands. (You may need some help at this stage to keep the leaves in position while putting the band in place.)

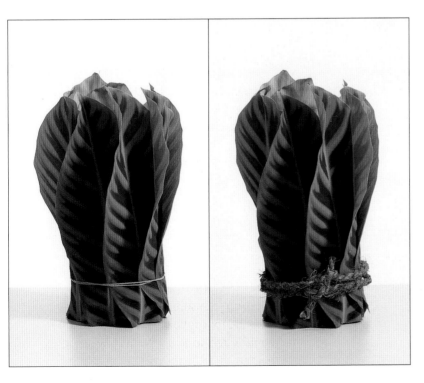

3 Carry on slipping leaves under the band, overlapping them so they all lie flat and in the same direction, until the whole container is covered. Tuck the last leaf under the first. Slip on a second elastic band to hold them all in place securely and trim the base of the leaves so that the vase can stand up. Tie rope or raffia over the elastic bands to hide them. In a suitable setting, matching or contrasting cord – even with one or two tassels – could be an elegant alternative.

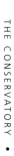

4 Fill the vase with water. Place three stems of lilies in the vase – one centrally and one at each side – so that they give you a guide for the height and width of the arrangement. When cutting them to length, keep in mind the overall shape you are creating and the proportions of the covered container.

5 Fill in the spaces with the remaining lilies, without hiding the tiger leaves around the container. Let the arrangement be open enough to show the shapes of the lily flowers – if it is too densely packed, the elegance of their silhouettes will be lost.

Index

Acknowledgements

Paul would like to thank Todd, Sue, Leonie, Jill, Susan, Neil, Barbara, Sarah, Jo and everyone at Paul Thomas Flowers in London for their excellent professional work and enthusiasm. A special word of thanks goes to Maureen and Derek Thomas and Sara and Callum for their constant support and appreciation. Last, and by no means least, thank you, Kenneth Turner, for being a superb teacher.

Jo would like to give her thanks to Malcolm and to Angie, to Stephani, Billy, Caroline and Jim, and all the friends who contributed their enthusiasm throughout the work – and of course to Ben, as ever, for putting up with everything. A special word to Helen Denholm for her friendship, for making it all happen and for sitting patiently through every photo shoot, despite the imminent birth of Katharine.

We would both like to express our gratitude to Guy Ryecart for his beautiful photography and outstanding dedication, along with Tony, his assistant. Our heartfelt thanks to Zoë Hughes, Rosemary Anderson, Caroline Hyams, Caroline Ball, Gail Engert and all the other people whose help and hard work have gone into this book. A word of acknowledgement to Jean Woolley, without whom we wouldn't have met, and to Heather Hollingshead, who also has a special place in our history.

Credits

PHOTOGRAPHIC CREDITS
Adams Picture Library 8/30–1; **Europa Photo Library** 94–5 (Girts Gailans); **John Glover** 10/20–1; **Jerry Harpur** 64–5, 74–5; **Images Colour Library** 6, 40–1; **Marianne Majerus** 116–17; **National Trust Photographic Library** 9/106–7 (Stephen Robson) 50–1 (Joe Cornish); **Tony Stone Images** 10–11 (Michael Bussell); **Juliette Wade** 84–5.

FLORAL AND OTHER SUPPLIES
Flowers, foliage and accessories came from a wide range of sources, including Paul Thomas's own shop, **Paul Thomas Flowers, 4 Shepherd Street, Mayfair, London W1Y 7LN (0171 499 6889)** and New Covent Garden Market. In addition:
Flowers: Peter and Tony at J. Ray Flowers Ltd, Dennis and Chris at John Austin Ltd, Alan at Alalar Ltd, Tony, David and Ian at Baker Duguid Ltd, Brian at Derek Hardcastle.
Foliage: David at John Egan and Sons Ltd, Barry and the team at Ronald Porter and Sons, David at A&F Bacon Ltd, Paul Thomas's own garden.
Plants: Arnot & Mason and Quality Plants, both at New Covent Garden.
Props: Pat at C. Best.
Sundries: Cocquerels Ltd.